An
APPROACH
to
St IGNATIUS of
LOYOLA

Michael Ivens SJ

edited by
Joseph A. Munitiz SJ

© *The Way*

First published 2008
by Way Books, Campion Hall,
Oxford, OX1 1QS
www.theway.org.uk

Cover Design: Peter Brook SJ

British Library Cataloguing-in-Publication Data
A catalogue record for this book is
available from the British Library

ISBN 978 0 904717 31 0

Printed by Hobbs the Printers Ltd, Totton, Hampshire

Contents

Editor's Preface

VERY EARLY IN HIS CAREER as a Jesuit, Michael Ivens, the author of the following pages, was imprudent enough to sign a contract with a publisher agreeing to write a 'life' of St Ignatius Loyola. He spent some time on the preliminary stages. However, the years went by; other projects took over; and finally illness intervened. The 'life' sank into oblivion.

After his death a few chapters emerged from his papers, and it is these that are now presented, hesitantly and with the caveats that are needed. Michael was a perfectionist; there are, for example, no fewer than three versions of the opening part of this short *Approach*, and it remains uncertain if he would have wanted any of these pages published. It must also be borne in mind that Michael was not a professional historian, and this work does not pretend to be the fruit of original research. Again, it is clear that these pages were written quite early in his career, before the deep reflective process that led to his main work, *Understanding the Spiritual Exercises*, had developed.

However, those who knew him will recognise flashes of his brilliance: the skill with which he marshals the information, the remarks that illuminate well-known facts, and the grace of his writing. All in all, this short account can serve as a first 'approach' to a person who dominated the thought and the life of Michael, and who deserves to be approached from many different angles.

Joseph A. Munitiz SJ

Abbreviations and References

All footnotes come from the original text, unless added in square brackets by the Editor.

Works by St Ignatius

Autobiography *Reminiscences, or Autobiography of Ignatius Loyola*, translated by Philip Endean, in St Ignatius of Loyola, *Personal Writings* (Harmondsworth: Penguin, 1996). Cited by paragraph number.

Exx *Spiritual Exercises*, cited by paragraph number. At this stage Michael was using one of the standard translations (probably that of Louis J. Puhl [Westminster, Md: Newman Press, 1951]); he later published his own translation (Gracewing and Inigo Enterprises, 2004).

Spiritual Diary *Spiritual Diary*, translated by Joseph A. Munitiz and Philip Endean, in St Ignatius of Loyola, *Personal Writings* (Harmondsworth: Penguin, 1996)

Other Works

Directories *On Giving the Spiritual Exercises: The Early Jesuit Manuscript Directories and the Official Directory of 1599*, edited by Martin E. Palmer SJ, (St Louis: Institute of Jesuit Sources, 1996).

Joseph de Guibert, *The Jesuits: their Spiritual Doctrine and Practice* (St Louis: Institute of Jesuit Sources, 1964), translation of *La spiritualité de la Compagnie de Jésus: Esquisse historique* (Rome: Institutum Historicum Societatis Jesu, 1953), used extensively in these pages.

1 Summary of a Life

Beginnings

THE CASTLE OF LOYOLA, a sheer-sided, functional building, without ornament except for an arabesque frieze below the upper storey and the family coat of arms over the main entrance, stands at the heart of the province of Guipúzcoa, some twenty miles south-west of the modern holiday resort of San Sebastián. There Iñigo López (only later would he assume the name of 'Ignatius' by which he is known to history) was born on an unknown date in 1491, the last of thirteen children of a family of Basque lesser nobility. Little is known of his early years. As a child he lost his mother, but the family was a close-knit one, and there is no reason to doubt that he passed a normal and happy childhood, under the tutelage of his sister-in-law, Magdalena, to whom he was devoted. In the Middle Ages it was the business of a landed family, such as that of Loyola, to furnish support to the Crown, both at home and abroad; and of the eight sons of Beltrán de Loyola, all except the second youngest, who became a priest, were involved, in one capacity or another, in the service of the Kings of Castile—two would be killed fighting with the Spanish forces in Naples, another would die in South America. As the cadet of the family, it was Iñigo who was originally set aside for the Church. At some point during his childhood he even received the tonsure, but in the event he entered the service of Juan Velázquez de Cuellar, Treasurer to the court of King Ferdinand, a beginning which would ordinarily have led to an administrative or political career.

He was thirteen when he took up his duties as a page in Velázquez's household at Arévalo, between Valladolid and Avila. It was an age in which a career in administration required little academic training, and his formal education was largely confined to reading and writing. Nevertheless, the years of adolescence and early adulthood at Arévalo gave him a style and culture that would mark him for life. He developed a passion for romantic fiction (as would the adolescent St Teresa three decades later in her father's house down the road at Avila). Partly through his reading and partly through the whole ethos of court life he imbibed the complex ambivalent and emotionally potent values of chivalry. From Arévalo, too, came the courtly style and easy dealings with the great personages of Church and State that would always characterize his behaviour. It was also in these years that he acquired a lifelong love of music.

There is not enough hard information for a detailed appraisal of his character at this time, but from the available evidence—much of it in Jesuit sources derived from Ignatius himself—certain broad traits emerge. While a staunchly orthodox and even pious Catholic— he detested blasphemy, abstained from music on Fridays, and would compose verses to the Blessed Virgin before a duel—his religion was essentially conventional. A Jesuit biographer observes discreetly that he was '*sat liber in mulierum amore*' ('somewhat free in his love of women'). All agree that he was physically vain and an addicted gambler. Ignatius himself in his *Autobiography*[1] identifies the ruling passion of his early life as 'the exercise of arms'. An item of evidence from the year 1521 helps to fill out these general impressions. Iñigo, with his priest brother, had been cited before the correctional court of Guipúzcoa for causing an affray in carnival time, and he had pleaded exemption from the court's jurisdiction on the grounds of his tonsure. But such a plea was admissible only if the accused had worn clerical attire for four months before the offence; whereas the accused in this case had 'worn long hair and multi-coloured garments, together with all the habiliments of a fighting man: coat of mail, breastplate, sword, musket and other kinds of arms'. In later life, Ignatius would look back on his years at Arévalo as a time of great scandal. The estimate must be taken seriously, for it was not his style to denigrate for effect. But whatever his faults, they were manifestly not those of a withdrawn, unromantic or pusillanimous personality; nor is there any reason to question the judgment of a Jesuit friend and confidant that in his formative years there was already in Ignatius a 'certain natural excellence ... a distaste for anything mean or common or within the scope of ordinary people'.

Iñigo remained with the Treasurer until the death of King Ferdinand and the succession of the initially unpopular Fleming, Charles V, in 1517. Under the new regime, Velázquez fell from favour and Iñigo was obliged to seek a new patron. Through the offices of

---

[1] [One version is easily available in St Ignatius of Loyola, *Personal Writings* (London: Penguin, 1996). Michael was using an earlier translation, and quotes extensively from it in the following pages.]

Velázquez's widow he obtained a place in the retinue of Antonio Manrique de Lara, the Duke of Nájera, whose prime responsibility at the time was the defence of Navarre, a territory newly annexed by Spain, unstable and vulnerable to attack from its former suzerain, France. The new situation there offered opportunities for the 'exercise of arms' that might never have arisen in the more domestic circumstances of the Treasurer's household. His first experience of a real military engagement probably occurred in 1521, when he took part in putting down an armed rebellion against the new king by the commons of Nájera. His conduct on that occasion was remembered chiefly for his refusal to participate in the pillage following the operation.

How far is it appropriate to describe Ignatius at this period of his life as a 'soldier'? The popular image of the soldier-turned-saint is not completely inapt. In his *Autobiography* he depicts himself in the early months of his conversion as a 'soldier of Christ'; and in the days before his conversion, he regarded a just fight as the ultimate in adventure and challenge ('just' meaning, in effect, consonant with feudal loyalty). *Joie de combat* is a concept he would certainly have understood. But it must be emphasized that by profession he was not a soldier but a feudal gentleman, whose duties included wide-ranging administrative and diplomatic responsibilities, as well as the obligation to bear arms when necessary on his lord's behalf. Evidence of his diplomatic activity comes from the year 1521 when he was one of a team of negotiators sent to Guipúzcoa to deal with a dispute over the appointment of a province governor, and he played a key role in bringing the factions to agreement.

A Jesuit biographer, Polanco,[2] would later claim that 'on many occasions, he proved his prudence and ingenuity in worldly affairs'; but the Guipúzcoa incident by itself proves that in his late twenties Ignatius possessed the intelligence and finesse of a diplomat. And the fact that he had once been a diplomat is quite as important a key to his later career as the fact that he had once been a soldier.

Pamplona and Loyola

Nevertheless, for the moment, the appeal of diplomacy came second to that of military adventure; for Ignatius aspired to the highest pinnacle of feudal 'honour' and only through distinction in arms could that be attained. That he possessed in full measure the audacity, powers of leadership and, above all, the physical courage necessary to achieve distinction in arms is clear from the unfolding of a brief military operation in May 1521, of negligible historical importance but crucially important in the personal life of Ignatius Loyola.

The French had launched the long-awaited invasion of Navarre. Iñigo and his elder brother, García, were summoned to the Navarrese capital, Pamplona, to reinforce the small body of the Duke's soldiers already in the city. They arrived to find a hopeless situation, with many of the Spanish troops in revolt, the majority of the town eager for surrender, and the new fortress, hastily constructed and still without battlement, in no state to withstand a siege. Iñigo's brother returned to

---

[2] [Juan Alfonso de Polanco (1517–1576); from 1547 he was secretary to Ignatius and became his right-hand man; a key figure in the early history of the Society, he wrote extensively on its early years.]

Guipúzcoa; Iñigo stayed behind to fight. When the attack on the fortress began, it was his electric quality that sustained the morale of the garrison,

> ... for though the others were for surrendering, he persuaded the governor by many reasons to carry on the defence against the judgement of all the knights. They found some strength in his spirit and courage (*Autobiography*,1).

However, in the course of the assault, Ignatius had his right knee crushed by a cannon-ball. With his fall, the defence of the fortress collapsed.

Field surgery and the seventy jolting miles back to Loyola on a litter must certainly have been an ordeal for Ignatius, but a far more severe ordeal awaited him at home. In the course of the journey, the bones in his leg had become displaced and the team of doctors summoned by his brother decided that the fracture must be set afresh. Ignatius withstood the operation— that 'butchery', he calls it—'without a word or any other sign of pain other than clenching his fists'—the only concession permitted by the code of chivalry. A complete physical collapse seems to have followed.

> He received the last sacraments on the feast of Saints Peter and Paul, when the doctors told him that if no improvement occurred by midnight, he could consider himself as good as dead.

Come midnight, however, he took a turn for the better, and within a few days was out of danger. But even now the ordeal was not over, for the wound had healed with one bone laying astride another, causing an unsightly protuberance. Could anything be done? A second operation, he was told, would cause greater and more prolonged agony than anything he had so far endured. His elder brother urged him to be sensible, 'for surely he would never have the courage to endure such pain'. But appalled by the thought of spending the rest of his life as a cripple, Ignatius 'to satisfy his own inclinations' bade the doctors set to work again. As flesh and bone were hacked away, 'he displayed the same fortitude as before'.

Conversion

It was during his convalescence from this surgery that Ignatius entered upon the first of three clearly demarcated inner transformations that, in little less than a year, would change the knightly careerist into a mystic —and, no less remarkably, a fledgling spiritual teacher.

To give his wound the best chance of healing, Ignatius was obliged to stay in bed even when he was out of pain and, apart from his injury, in good health. As the summer months wore on, he became desperately bored. He asked for novels to while away the time. But the only books to be found in the house were two religious ones: the four-volume *Life of Christ* by the fourteenth-century Carthusian Ludolf of Saxony, and a work of hagiology, a medieval best-seller, variously known as the *Golden Legend* and the *Flower of the Saints*, written by a Dominican, James of Varazze. The latter had been translated into Spanish and supplemented by additional materials by a Cistercian monk named Vergad, who had formerly followed a career similar to that of Ignatius. These books, in default of romantic novels, Ignatius began to read.

They did not change his life at a stroke, for even without romantic novels he could still indulge in romantic day-dreams, and for hours on end he would lie thinking about 'a lady of no ordinary rank, neither a duchess nor a countess, but far higher than these', and about 'the means he would take to reach the land where she lived, the verses he would compose in her honour, the deeds of gallantry he would perform in her service'. But in time the lives of the saints began to catch his imagination too, leading him to explore new avenues of adventure. In his fantasies, their heroic achievements seemed attractive and within reach. 'His only thought was to tell himself: "St Francis did this, so must I"; "St Dominic did this, therefore I must do the same".' For a time he was pulled in two directions, until gradually he became aware of a curious and consistent difference between the ways his conflicting dreams were affecting him.

> When he was thinking of the things of the world, he was filled with delight, but when he had dismissed them from weariness, he was dry and dissatisfied. But when he thought of performing the rigours he saw in the lives of the saints, he was not only consoled while he entertained the thoughts, but even afterwards he remained cheerful and satisfied.

As he dwelt on the difference and sought an explanation, he became aware that something more significant was going on than mere day-dreaming, and that the contrasting moods—dryness and disenchantment on the one hand, and on the other a quality of peace and joy strangely different from anything he had previously known—could only be the working of two opposite 'spirits', 'the one from the demon, the other from God'.

This insight, later to develop into a highly sophisticated teaching on the 'discernment of spirits', but at this stage intuitive and uncomplicated, marks the real starting-point of his conversion. Peace and joy gradually became a settled mental climate. In this mood, the past took on a new aspect, its achievements and satisfactions appearing now superficial and gross. As he recalled this time over the retrospect of thirty years, one incident in particular stood out: the night when he lay awake and 'saw clearly the likeness of Our Lady and the Holy Child', and experienced 'so great a distaste for his past life, especially for the things of the flesh, that it was as though the images graven on his mind vanished'. As he got up and moved about the house, he divided his time between prayer, reading and transcribing excerpts from the Gospels into a notebook; while at night he would gaze at the stars, 'feeling within himself a powerful urge to serve God'.

Meanwhile, the vision of a new future, at first glimpsed in day-dreams, came to crystallize about three clear intentions. As soon as he was well enough to travel, he would go to Jerusalem as a pilgrim. Both during and after his pilgrimage, he would follow a regime of severe physical asceticism modelled on the most austere examples he could find in the lives of the saints. And, like St Francis, he would embrace a radical ideal of poverty, living as a beggar and vagrant—a prospect that held more attraction for him than the briefly considered alternative of joining the Carthusians.

In February 1522 he set out on his travels, intending to reach the Holy Land with as little delay as possible. For this he needed to go to Barcelona, the port of embarkation for Italy; and his plans included a brief visit to the Benedictine monastery of Montserrat, well known in court circles both for its ancient black Madonna and as a centre of learning and spiritual reform. In the course of the journey a bizarre incident occurred concerning a Moorish fellow-traveller, with whom Ignatius got the worst of an argument about the virginity of Mary. In the *Autobiography* he recalls what happened: how the Moor pulled ahead, leaving him frustrated and angry; how he considered overtaking the Moor and vindicating Our Lady's honour with a dagger thrust; how his own mule eventually resolved the issue by taking another road than the highway leading to the Moor's village. Later he would recognise his reactions for what they were—a recrudescence of the old quarrelsome self under the guise of chivalrous piety—and he would realise how absurdly remote they were from the words he had so devotedly copied out into his notebook. But at the time he was content to have done what seemed best. Buoyant and peaceful again, he resumed his thoughts about 'the great deeds he would do for God'. The next incident he records was the purchase of a pilgrim's staff, a gourd, and a piece of loose-woven sackcloth 'with a rough and prickly surface', which he had made up into a garment.

Montserrat and Manresa

At Montserrat he was placed under the charge of a learned and saintly French monk named Chanon, who taught him to prepare for confession with the help of a book, the *Exercitatory of the Spiritual Life*, by the former abbot of the monastery, García Cisneros. After three days he made a confession of his entire life. Then, on the eve of the Annunciation, after putting on his pilgrim garb and donating his fine clothes to a beggar, he spent the entire night 'without ever sitting or lying down, but now standing now kneeling before the altar of Our Lady'. The idea had come to him during his journey from Loyola, while he had been thinking of his favourite novel, *Amadís de Gaul*. But to dismiss it as a piece of chivalrous whimsy would be to misunderstand Ignatius' situation. Chivalry had been the driving inspiration of his life, and he had now to go beyond the limitations of chivalry, while deepening and redirecting everything genuine in it. In these circumstances, to have bade farewell to his arms, finery and all they stood for in his own recycled version of a knightly investiture, was probably a gesture of some spiritual and psychological importance, in its way putting a seal on the healing and renovation he had found in the sacrament.

If there is one place, after Loyola, with which Ignatius' name is inseparably connected, it is the small town of Manresa at the foot of the Montserrat range, where he spent a period of ten months which he would later describe as his 'primitive Church'. Precisely why, on leaving the monastery, he did not proceed straight to Barcelona, according to his original plan, is not known. Possibly it was too late to reach Rome in time to get permission to go to the Holy Land that year. Possibly, after the heart-searching at Montserrat and his conversations with Chanon, he felt the need for a period of regular, stable and penitential life before taking to the road again. At all events, it was to such a life that he now gave himself.

He found lodging first in a hospital and later with the Dominicans; by day he would retire to a cave for solitude. Every day he attended mass and vespers, and prayed for seven hours on his knees, rising at night. He lived on alms, and as he made his way about the town with his begging bowl he became a familiar figure of amusement to the street children, who quickly found a name for him: 'The man in the sack'. He fasted on a scale that would permanently undermine his health. To punish his vanity he deliberately neglected his appearance, letting his hair and fingernails grow anyhow. In the intervals between prayer and begging he would reread the excerpts in his notebook, and pore over the pages of another book he discovered at this time, the *Imitation of Christ*. It seems likely that from time to time he went back to Montserrat. And for some months his 'interior state of great and steady happiness' continued.

Crisis

When he came to recall this period in his *Autobiography*, two things were clear to Ignatius. First, his conversion was absolutely genuine. In no sense was he caught up in the vaporous euphoria of a person who has 'got religion'. He was *encendido de Dios* ('on fire for God') and filled with the desire 'to serve God to the best of his knowledge'. Everything a man of his background could recognise as sin he had totally repudiated; and the ideal of sanctity, as far as he was capable of understanding it, was now his overriding ambition. But he also saw himself as far less spiritually mature than he had thought himself to be at the time. There was something callow, even unconsciously egocentric, about his obsession with 'great external deeds'. In particular, the incident with the Moor served to highlight his deficiency in the deeper spiritual qualities, such as 'humility, charity, and patience, to say nothing of discretion as the rule and measure of these virtues'. He was in fact at the stage of intense, but slightly adolescent, fervour which is a common sequel to decisive conversion. And it is generally recognised that the very intensity of this experience has a double effect: on the one hand it consolidates the convert's newly acquired values, and on the other it protects him against more challenging ones that he is not yet ready for. Hence first fervour tends to produce a deceptive sense of completion. Moreover, in Ignatius' case, both the fervour and the deception must have been endorsed by his own make-up and culture—the penchant for the heroic that was second nature to him long before his conversion, and the influence of chivalrous ideology with its insistence on the 'great deed' in itself as the touchstone of personal worth.

Had he remained at this stage of growth, Ignatius might have been remembered—if at all—as a romantic religious eccentric in an age in which religious eccentrics abounded. What cleared the way to further development was the experience—for him severe and prolonged—of the darkening of vision and collapse of emotional support that he would describe in the *Exercises* as 'desolation'. His emotional life, previously aglow with the divine presence, became suddenly arid, so that even in prayer and mass he found no relish. The future no longer offered exhilarating prospects of 'great things for God', and became instead bleak and menacing, 'as if a voice were saying within his soul, "How can you carry on like this for the seventy years you may yet have to live?"'. He fell prey to the anxieties known as 'scruples', which can be—and in Ignatius' case were—one of the most searing forms of mental suffering imaginable. Repeatedly, he would go back over old ground in confession without finding relief; and when his confessor forbade him to mention past sins again 'unless there was something absolutely clear', the advice proved useless, 'since to him everything was clear'. In the *Autobiography* he describes the long plunge into near-despair as the months of suffering wore on:

> While these thoughts were tormenting him, he was frequently seized with the temptation to throw himself into an excavation close to his room ... but knowing it was a sin to do away with himself, he cried out again, 'Lord, I will do nothing to offend you!'.

But what brought deliverance in the end was neither fasting nor the endless attempts to achieve the impossibly comprehensive confession. The end when it came was 'like being awakened from a dream by God'. As peace came flooding back, he decided very firmly not to confess anything from the past any more; and 'from that day forward he remained free of those scruples and held it for certain that God in his mercy had wished to deliver him'.

How is this crisis to be explained? One explanation comes readily to mind. Ignatius had been living at a pitch that even he could not possibly have sustained. What more natural than that he should have been over-taken by nervous exhaustion inducing severe depression?

Indeed something of that kind may have been happening. But Ignatius, who at the time of dictating his *Autobiography* was familiar with the concept of 'melancholy', is quite clear that the crisis was essentially a crisis of spiritual growth. Such a crisis may, it must be added, be occasioned by a situation of great stress, and it may also produce temporary effects similar to those of psychological breakdown. And though Ignatius in the *Autobiography* is mainly concerned to narrate his experience rather than analyze it, the deep significance of the graphically sketched details will be clear to any reader possessing some acquaintance with mystical literature: the impression of being abandoned by God; an overwhelming sense of sin; powerlessness to attain peace and consolation through any efforts of one's own; unremitting fidelity to prayer in spite of aridity; and the anxiety-laden concern to do nothing to offend God. All this is typical of a phenomenon repeatedly described in the literature of mysticism: the 'night' or 'desert' in which an already generous desire for God is further strengthened and purified, and the mind and will made receptive for a new transforming action of the Holy Spirit.

Enlightenment

With the resolution of this crisis, Ignatius' life passed, after a brief period of dawning, into the third stage of his conversion, which may be described as that of enlightenment. In his own image, he entered upon a process of mystical education (though here as in all his writings he conveys the concept of mysticism while avoiding the word itself):

> God treated him at this time as a schoolmaster treats
> a young scholar. Whether this was on account of his
> coarseness or his dense intelligence, or because he
> had no one to teach him, or because of the strong
> desire God himself had given him to serve Him, he
> clearly believed, and has always believed, that God
> treated him in this way.

In the *Autobiography* the main elements of this
education are summarised in a list of five intellectual
visions, or enlightenments. The first of these occurred
while he was reciting the Office of Our Lady on the
steps of a monastery, waiting for the start of one of the
processions that were a favourite feature in the religious
life of the town. As he prayed,

> ... his mind began to be elevated, it was as though
> he beheld the Holy Trinity under the form of three
> keys of a musical instrument, and weeping and
> sobbing so overcame him that he could not control
> himself.

Still in floods of tears, he tacked himself on to the
procession, doubtless impervious to what people might
be making of the latest behaviour of 'the man in the
sack'.

But if for a time the wonder of the Trinity completely absorbed him, that was only the beginning of his
education. From the contemplation of the Trinity in
itself, he moved in the second vision to contemplating
the work of the Trinity:

> On another occasion, there was represented to his
> understanding, with great spiritual delight, the
> manner in which God had created the world. He

had a vision of something white, out of which rays were coming, and it was out of this that God created light.

The third and fourth visions had to do with the presence within the world of the risen and glorified Christ, in the sacrament and in the situations of daily life:

> When he was hearing mass in the church of the monastery already mentioned, during the elevation he saw with the inner eyes of the soul something like white rays coming from above. Though he cannot explain after so long a time, what he clearly saw with his understanding was how Jesus Christ our Lord is present in the most holy sacrament .... At times of prayer, he often and for a long time saw with the inner eyes the humanity of Christ. The shape that appeared to him was like a white body, not very large or very small, but he saw no distinction of members. He often saw this at Manresa.

The fifth and culminating experience came about one day in September while he was taking a walk to a church about a mile outside the town. 'The road ran alongside the little river' (the Cardoner), and after walking part of the way, he sat down with his face towards the water, 'which at that point was running deep'. There in an experience transcending sense and imagery, his mind was opened in a single comprehensive intuition:

> He beheld no vision but he saw and understood many things, matters spiritual as well as those

concerning faith and theology. There was so great an illumination that these things appeared altogether new.

Ignatius was sparing of literary adornment but profoundly sensitive to the power of symbols: 'deep water' conveys as aptly as any language the intensification of life, the breakthrough into a new lucidity that Ignatius experienced. Nor is it merely accidental that he remembers so vividly that he had encountered the Spirit 'on the road': roads, on which he was to spend so much of his life, fascinated him. They stood for the nobility, insecurity, and exposure of the pilgrim condition; and throughout his life it was as a man of the road that he was to be guided and sustained by the grace of contemplation.

What Ignatius really experienced in this time of enlightenment, and particularly in the vision beside the Cardoner, and how the experience changed him, he could never adequately convey. The essential was not in the oddly tenuous imagery—'keys of a musical instrument', 'something white', etc.—nor in the powerful accompanying emotions, nor even in the conceptual content, but in an illumination of mind, which of its nature is incommunicable, and which he admits he himself could not completely recapture. Nevertheless, certain things are clear. Though he learned nothing that on one level he did not know already (technical theology would come later), the insights received at Manresa amounted to a qualitatively new way of knowing: 'he has often thought that even were there no Scriptures to teach us these matters of faith, he would die for them on account of what he had seen'. Quite certainly, it was in the experience of Manresa that the main lines of his future theological outlook were laid down: the dominance of the Trinity, the central place of the humanity of Christ, the sense of the world as God's creation and gift. And there is no doubt that the experience transformed him at the very core of his selfhood. It was a uniquely decisive event, which left him, in the words of Nadal,[3] 'a new man, with a new mind, a new will, a new appreciation of all things', and in later years he would frequently justify his decisions and attitudes simply by referring to 'something that happened in the town of Manresa'.

After the vision of the Cardoner, Ignatius remained at Manresa for a further four or five months, and during this time the effects of his new outlook appear in two ways.

First draft of the *Spiritual Exercises*

It was in these months that he roughed out the initial draft of the *Spiritual Exercises*. Over the years, study and further experience would lead him to revise and expand the book considerably, but it is certain that the sheaf of papers with which he left Manresa already contained the essentials of the future classic, including the fundamental meditations known as the 'Kingdom' and the 'Two Standards'. Ignatius would always insist that the *Exercises* arose not from book-learning, but out

---

[3] [Jerónimo Nadal (1507–80) met Ignatius in Paris (1534) and reacted against him; only in 1545 did he undergo a change of heart and enter the new order, becoming a key player in its expansion, and chosen by Ignatius with the delicate task of explaining the newly written *Constitutions* all over Europe. He urged Ignatius to dictate his *Autobiography*.]

of the stuff of his own life. This is not, of course, to deny that they also owe something to immediate influences. To some extent—though precisely how far is difficult to determine—he had been touched by the *devotio moderna*,[4] as taught and practised at Montserrat. He had also been influenced by the books he had read: the *Life of Christ*, the *Golden Legend*, the *Imitation of Christ*, the *Exercitatorio* of Cisneros, and perhaps some others as well. Nevertheless, the *Exercises* are marked by qualities of penetration and insight beyond anything, with the possible exception of the *Imitation*, that Ignatius had so far read, and they are quite unlike the *Imitation* in style, structure and indeed in doctrinal emphasis. The *Exercises* came to birth, certainly, in a given cultural context, but the key to their distinctive content and spirit is to be found not so much in external sources as in his own inner journey, reflected upon and interpreted in the light of a wisdom of his own.

The pilgrim

At the same time as the text of the *Exercises* was taking shape, changes appear in Ignatius' behaviour and practical attitudes. In response to a vision and an accompanying 'strong movement of the spirit', he started to eat meat again, even though his confessor, disconcerted perhaps by his penitent's new-found confidence, suggested that the impulse might be a temptation. For some time, intense spiritual feelings had been keeping him awake at night; now he decided to ignore the feelings and give

---

[4] [A spiritual movement that spread from the Netherlands and found expression in a series of publications, notably the writings of the Flemish mystics and Thomas à Kempis, with great stress on personal prayer and lay involvement.]

the appointed time to sleep. 'He saw the fruitfulness of his work for souls'—the simple ministry of instruction and spiritual conversation, to which he now devoted an increasing amount of time. So as to be more acceptable to other people, he abandoned his desert-father habits and trimmed his hair and fingernails. In the severe winter of 1522 he fell seriously ill, and friends in the town lovingly but firmly took charge of him:

> He was treated with great attention, and many prominent ladies out of affection for him came to watch over him by night. Though he recovered from this sickness, he was still very weak and frequently suffered from stomach-pains. For these reasons, therefore, and because the winter was very cold, they made him dress better and wear shoes and cover his head; they made him wear two brown doublets of very coarse cloth and a bonnet of the same stuff, a kind of beret.

It is hard to imagine that Ignatius gave way to this cosseting without some token resistance; but only a few weeks previously it would have taken the direct orders of his confessor to budge him from any point of his self-imposed ascetical programme!

Significantly, the changes of behaviour he ascribes to his time of enlightenment are all, in fact, modifications of his former ascetical programme. In themselves, the details are trivial enough—shoes, a beret, warm clothes, trimmed hair and fingernails, regular sleep and an occasional meat meal; but taken together, they pinpoint the deep changes of outlook that separate the first from the last stage of Ignatius' 'primitive Church'. He is now less an imitator and more an individual, with a mind and heart of his own, and a new Spirit-given sense of the appropriate. Though the hero is still alive and well, the obstinacy has gone out of his heroism. He no longer regards material things as snares to be avoided, but as gifts to be used. There is a place in his new outlook for kindness, as well as rigour, towards the body. And asceticism is no longer the largely private affair that it had been for the raw convert, burning with the desire for 'disciplines and abstinences'; but a vision is beginning to open in which everything, asceticism included, is ordered to the service of the kingdom of God in the world. When he left the castle of Loyola for the first step of his Jerusalem journey, many expressions might have been found to epitomize his spiritual outlook, but it could hardly be claimed that he was living out a spirituality of 'finding God in all things'. A year later, as he is about to take to the road again, the description is beginning to fit.

During his convalescence, Ignatius reached one quite definite resolution: to make a pilgrimage to Jerusalem and to live out the remainder of his days in the land made sacred by his Lord. On 8 July 1523 he embarked from Venice for Palestine. It was a short-lived venture. With Palestine under Muslim rule, life was dangerous for a lone permanent pilgrim such as Ignatius desired to be; and, afraid for his safety, the Franciscan guardians of the Holy Places sent him home after three weeks. Yet Ignatius' account of this time makes illuminating reading for the student of his spirituality. He tells how, in defiance of human prudence, he insisted on making the journey penniless, so as to experience as profoundly as possible his dependence on providence. He describes how he bribed the Turkish guards to be allowed to return alone to Mount Olivet to examine in closer detail marks on a rock allegedly made by the feet of Christ. He recounts how, in conversation with the Franciscan Provincial, he had pressed his reasons for staying in Palestine, and how he had acceded to the Provincial's contrary judgment on learning that the latter was empowered to excommunicate anyone who refused his authority:

> ... as the Provincial was willing to show him the Bulls, the pilgrim said that there was no need of his seeing them, since he believed their references, and since they so judged with the authority conferred on them, he would obey.

Searching for a way

He returned to Spain in the hope that eventually he might still return to Jerusalem; but the immediate goal of his pilgrimage changes. The concern that now dominates his mind springs from a discovery made at the very outset of his new way of life, when even in the solitude and spiritual rawness of his early days, people flocked to him for spiritual counsel, and he had realised that wisdom in the ways of God could never be simply a treasured private possession. So his quest now is to discover the most effective means to 'help souls'. It was to be a daunting search, but it must begin, clearly, with study. He therefore studied Latin under a Barcelona schoolmaster and, armed with the bare rudiments of the language, he proceeded to the university of Alcalá, where, in blissful disregard for the demands of serious study, he seems to have wandered from one course to another. Meanwhile, with four young companions (who did not eventually remain with him), he continued his apostolate on the lines that had already emerged at Manresa. Spiritual conversation—an art he was to cherish and advocate to the end of his life—loomed large in the programme. In addition he taught Christian doctrine and, when appropriate, gave the First Week of the Exercises to a clientele consisting of children, devout ladies, the poor, and the small shopkeepers who provided him with alms, meeting places and occasional lodging.

It was probably inevitable that pastoral activity of this sort on the part of a layman with scant academic qualifications should have aroused the suspicions of the Inquisition. Twice Ignatius was imprisoned, at Alcalá and at Salamanca. On each occasion, while his doctrine was declared free from error, his liberty to teach was subjected to hampering restrictions, and on each occasion he moved on, in the hope of finding freedom in another ecclesiastical territory. It must be admitted that, judged by their own harsh standards, the Inquisitors were not unduly severe with Ignatius; indeed one is left with the impression that, while he certainly caused them anxiety, it was an anxiety tempered with respect. Ignatius, on his side, acknowledged the authority of the Inquisitors, but also their limitations. He regarded their decisions in his regard as unfair; and while he complied within the bounds of duty, there is a noticeable difference in tone between his dealings with the Inquisition and with the Franciscan Provincial at Jerusalem.

Here, for instance, is an exchange between Ignatius and the Vicar, Figueroa, whom the Toledo Inquisition had put in charge of Ignatius' case. The Pilgrim, as he now refers to himself, promised to follow his instructions

[Figueroa had instructed Ignatius and his companions, since they were not religious, to dye their clothes different colours]:

> But I do not know what use there is in these investigations. Just a few days ago a certain priest refused to give one of us communion, because he received every week, and they have even made it difficult for me. We should like to know whether we have been found in some heresy. 'No', answered Figueroa, 'For if they had they would burn you'. 'They would burn you too', rejoined the Pilgrim, 'if they found you in heresy.'

Describing his appearance before the court at Salamanca, which forbade him to distinguish between mortal and venial sin, he writes:

> When the sentence was read, the judges gave signs of great affection, as though they wished to see it accepted. The Pilgrim said that he would do all that the sentence required of him, but that he would not accept it, because without condemning him on any point, they closed his mouth to prevent his helping his neighbour in what he could. No matter how much the Doctor Frías, who showed great friendliness, urged the matter, the Pilgrim said that as long as he was in the jurisdiction of Salamanca, he would do as the sentence bade him.

It was as a direct consequence of this sentence that Ignatius made the fateful decision in 1524 to continue his studies in Paris.

Paris

The Paris years are profoundly important in the genesis of Ignatius' spirituality, not so much because they bring qualitatively new developments, as because many nascent characteristics of his mature outlook acquire direction and momentum at this time.

First of all, his spiritual development gained much from the hard experience of life as a 'mature student', faced with the double handicap of a neglected education and scant financial resources. Realising that in Spain 'he had hurried too quickly from grammar to higher studies', he went back to the beginning, putting himself to school with nine-year-old boys. The pinch of poverty was a terrible hindrance and, having failed to find employment as a college servant, he fell back on making begging tours during the long vacations. Study was further impeded by the multitude of spiritual considerations 'which arose in his mind while the master was lecturing', but in this phenomenon he had no difficulty now in recognising the subtle wiles of the angel of darkness. The student years, in short, confirm a development in Ignatius' outlook which began in the early stages of his conversion, a development which might be defined as a progress from the asceticism of the desert to the asceticism of the apostle. At Manresa he had greatly admired a rugged desert saint called Onuphrius, and he had vied with this hero in producing exploits of imprudence and hardship: 'led by sincere intentions', he later admitted,

> ... he reckoned that holiness was entirely measured by exterior austerity of life and that he who did the most severe penances would be held in the divine

estimation for the most holy, an idea which made him determine to lead a very harsh life.

He emerged from Paris with his capacity for hardship undiminished, but with a settled appreciation of the subtler asceticism of finding God's will in the exigencies of practical realities.

At Paris he became, too, a competent, though not a learned, academic theologian. True, there is an intuitive as well as an acquired element in the confident grasp of doctrine which, before Paris as well as afterwards, enabled him to emerge unscathed from the most rigorous official scrutiny. But even if he never became a man of learning, it would be far from the truth to place him among the saints who have relied mainly on inspired but untutored insight. It was his theological formation that enabled him, during the Paris years, to impart to a number of sections of the *Exercises* their definitive theological formulation; and for the rest of his life, his thought was to bear the impress of the scholastic theology he imbibed at Paris.

He was affected for life, too, by his encounter at first hand with the Reformation. Raging controversy, the sense of traditional values under threat, the savage—and never wholly successful—persecution of heretics: these formed the ambience of Ignatius' student life. Whereas in Spain he seems to have been little concerned with the ill-defined movement known as 'illuminism' (in spite of being suspected of complicity in it), in Paris it was impossible to be anything but acutely aware that the religious world was violently divided. The experience confirmed Ignatius definitively in the intransigent stance towards heretics, as well as towards heresy, which was to remain a hallmark of his personality. His wholehearted approval of the draconian heresy laws of the time is a trait we find today impossible to stomach, but at least we can try to understand his attitude towards heresy itself, as evidenced in the uncompromising, but not unbalanced, 'Rules for thinking with the Church'. Heresy, in his view, was an assault on the very means of salvation; and its effect on souls was incalculable and uncontrollable—rather like contaminating the public water supply. While it would be false to claim that he founded his Order expressly in order to counter the Reformation, he was certainly preoccupied throughout his life by the reformers' challenge to the Church. The defence of Catholic orthodoxy and of the Church's authority was always to be dominant among his concerns:

> If we wish to proceed securely in all things, we must hold fast to the following principle: what seems to me white, I will believe black if the hierarchical Church so defines. For I must be convinced that in Christ our Lord, the bridegroom and in his spouse the Church, one Spirit holds sway, which governs and rules for the salvation of souls. For it is by the same Spirit and Lord, who gave the Ten Commandments, that our holy Mother Church is ruled and governed. (Exx 365)

But it would also be false to imagine that to Ignatius' mind the dividing line between orthodoxy and heresy was always clear, or that head-on conflict was always the best way to serve the former. In an atmosphere of controversy, it was easy to overreact, to lose sight of the nuance, to hear things in one sense that were meant in another. There were times, then, when the truth was best served by reticence.[5] While these careful statements are biased, as might be expected, towards the Catholic side of the great controversies of the day, they reflect, too, Ignatius' awareness that imbalance on the Catholic side is also a possibility.

Finally, it was in Paris that Ignatius won over his room-mates, Francis Xavier [Francisco Javier] and Peter Faber [Pierre Favre] and, with these and four others, formed the group of friends who were eventually to found the Society of Jesus. It is impossible to read the companions' later descriptions of this group without catching a sense of nostalgia, the remembrance of almost impossibly happy and uncomplicated relationships. Diego Laínez (future General of the Society) recalls, for instance, that:

> On certain days we would go to eat in the dwelling first of one and then of another, bringing our own food. This, together with frequent other visits and spiritual conversations, helped us a great deal to persevere. The Lord gave us special help in our studies, in which we made good progress, dedicating them always to the glory of God and the good of our neighbour. He helped us particularly by joining us together in fervent mutual love, and we used also to aid each other materially as far as we could.[6]

---

[5] Rules 14–17 of the Rules for Thinking with the Church can be cited here (Exx 366–369).

[6] [Diego Laínez, letter, 16 June 1547, published in Spanish and Latin in *Monumenta Historica Societatis Iesu*, 66 (included as document 6 in the *Fontes Narrativi Sancti Ignatii*, volume 1, 102–103) (Rome: Jesuit Historical Institute, 1943).]

The group was, in short, a conspicuously successful example of the sort of association that flourishes readily on university soil; association based upon common religious ideals and nourished by mutual support in study and by the rituals of friendship. As opportunity offered, and the companions proved ready for the experience, Ignatius gave them, singly and in solitude, the Spiritual Exercises. On 15 August 1534, in a chapel on the hillside of Montmartre, the group of seven set the seal of their dedication to Christ and to one another by pronouncing vows of poverty and chastity, together with a third vow to go to the Holy Land. Should the pilgrimage prove impossible, they would offer themselves to the Pope for any work or mission to which he might assign them.

Foundation of the Society of Jesus

Before the idea arose of setting up a new religious order, five more pilgrim years were to elapse. During this time the companions would travel, make further studies in theology, receive ordination and, as an official community of 'reformed priests', gain their first systematic experience of active ministry. In order to understand the novel and distinctive character of the Society it is necessary to start, then, by looking at the lifestyle and activity of the companions in the years immediately preceding the Society's foundation.

They were a group which continued to depend heavily on personal bonds. Though living together was an occasional luxury rather than a regular practice, they maintained the close association that had characterized the student group. It was their habit when possible to work and travel in pairs or threes. Decisions were reached through common deliberation based upon prayer. They lived on alms and fended for themselves, often precariously. Here, for instance, is Ignatius' account of the pre-ordination retreat at Vicenza, which he shared with Favre and Laínez:

> There [in Vicenza] they found a house outside the city limits, which had neither door nor window, where they slept on a little straw they brought with them. Two of the three went twice daily to ask for alms, and brought back so little that they could hardly subsist. Usually they ate a little toasted bread, when they had it, prepared by the one whose lot it was to remain at home. In this manner they spent forty days intent on nothing but their prayer.

It was at this period that Rodríguez, making his own retreat fifty miles away at Bassano, fell sick; and Ignatius, though himself unwell at the time, set off with Favre to visit him, 'setting such a pace that his companion could hardly keep up'. Concern for one another's health is, indeed, a prominent characteristic of the group. When at the end of his time in Paris, Ignatius had been ordered by the doctors to return to Spain for 'native air', the companions had bought him a small horse and persuaded him to abandon his usual practice of travelling on foot.

Their activities were highly diversified. While the ultimate aim was simply the service of Christ, the means included any type of ministry within their competence. They worked in prisons and hospitals. They plunged into theological controversy. They taught the rudiments of doctrine to street children. They preached in churches and market squares. In the severe Roman winter of 1536–8 they made their mark on the city by bedding down homeless people, a hundred at a time, in the allegedly haunted house they had acquired as a base. The first years in Rome saw, too, the first institutions to be founded by Ignatius: a house for reformed prostitutes, a centre for Jewish catechumens, and a free school for boys.

It was also a group which aimed to foster in its members a common spiritual ideal. But their way of life left little room for either the regularity or the ascetical observances of monastic life, so rules were of the simplest: daily meditation and examination of conscience; weekly confession and communion; a weekly—and later monthly—change of superior. The shape of life was largely determined by the claims of the apostolate: the constant preaching and instruction, travel, and the service of the destitute. And it was precisely this that made the life one of formidable rigour. The demands of service made inroads into everything, leaving time neither for proper sleep nor for the adequate preparation of sermons and lectures. The record of their journeys and ministries is peppered, too, with grim little vignettes: Ignatius crawling on all fours across the Apennines crippled by stomach ache; the companions staving off hunger by eating pine cones; Francis Xavier licking pus from his fingers 'to overcome the rebellion of nature' against the squalid conditions of the Renaissance hospitals.

During the years immediately preceding the Society's foundation, the companions experienced, then, the cost of discipleship that they had pondered in the *Spiritual Exercises*. They discovered that to share in Christ's 'enterprise' was to be with Christ in poverty, toil, hunger and abuse. They had proved that in such conditions Christ could be met, known and loved. They had discovered a style of association close enough to afford mutual strength and encouragement, yet loose enough to meet the missionary's need for freedom of movement. They were clear too that this way of life was profoundly different from that of any established form of religious life, and that to join an existing order would put an end to 'our fondest dreams, conceived, as we believe, under God's inspiration'.

The process by which the group came to establish a new order—and with it a new form of religious life— can be briefly summarised. In 1538, the companions made their way to Rome (and it was on this journey that Ignatius received his second decisive revelation at La Storta[7]). Owing to the outbreak of war with the Turkish empire, the Jerusalem project finally foundered, and the alternative vow came into effect. Accordingly, the companions offered themselves to Paul III, 'the lord of Christ's universal harvest', undertaking to do whatever work, and to go 'without delay or excuse' to whatever place the man with the widest knowledge of the Church's needs would consider best—whether 'to the Turks or the New World, to the Lutherans or to any others, whether Christians or infidels'. The offer was soon to be taken up: first in Italy—'that will be a true and good Jerusalem', the Pope had said—and before long as far afield as India, the companions found themselves working at the Pope's behest. This dispersal,

---

[7] [Michael intended to elaborate on this La Storta incident, but nothing has survived.]

with its threat of dissolution for the loosely structured group, led in turn to further developments. In 1539, after much deliberation, they agreed unanimously to retain their mutual ties, even in conditions of dispersal, and to strengthen those ties by the adoption of the third of the traditional religious vows, 'obedience to one of our own number'. By doing so they took the decisive step towards the establishment of a new religious order. In 1540, the Bull of foundation was issued. In the following year, Ignatius was elected General Superior. For the remaining years of his life, the Pilgrim became desk-bound, devoting his time to the administration of the Society and to writing its *Constitutions*. When he died in 1556 the group of student friends had grown to an order of over a thousand members.

2 Major Works

The *Spiritual Exercises*

PEOPLE WHO READ THE *EXERCISES* with no previous knowledge of their nature and purpose usually come away with the feeling that, if there is a treasure here, it resides in a decidedly earthen vessel. At first sight the book turns out to be little more than a collection of notes. If an occasional phrase suggests the mind, though never the language, of a poet, the overall impression is one of stark angularity; and the casual reader finds little of the immediate inspiration that might be expected of a popular classic. What, then, is the secret of the astonishing success of the *Exercises* over four centuries? How are we to account for their increasing vogue in our own theologically sophisticated times?

The answer hinges upon the fact that the *Exercises* were intended not to be 'read', but to be 'made'. To make these 'exercises' is to embark upon a personal adventure in the ways of the Spirit: an adventure leading to the renewal of mind and heart; to a 'deep-felt knowledge and love of God our Lord made man for me'; to a Spirit-given strength to walk the road of service with Christ in peace and joy. To achieve this end, Ignatius mapped out a general route divided into four stages or 'weeks'. He begins with a highly concise theological statement of the ultimate purpose of man and the world (the 'Principle and Foundation'), and then proceeds in the First Week to the theme of conversion. The Second Week is devoted to the contemplation of the life of Christ, with special emphasis on sharing the labour and poverty of Christ's missionary life. In the Third and Fourth Weeks the exercitant is conducted through the suffering and death of Christ to the glory and joy of the resurrection. And the whole is rounded off with the celebrated 'Contemplation for Attaining Love' (probably composed in Paris), where Ignatius adumbrates the kind of prayer in which a person reconciled to God might contemplate God in the whole of creation.

But if there is a constant underlying plan in the *Exercises*, the adventure of making them is always personal and unique. Some have a stormy passage, others a relatively tranquil one. Frequently the experience centres upon a serious and difficult personal decision, but it may serve equally to confirm and deepen an already existing commitment. The ways of the spirit are unpredictable and hence these 'exercises' were to be made following not the prescriptions of a book, but the personal guidance of a director. The role of the director is delineated by Ignatius with considerable care. He or she must explain, apply, and when necessary adjust the Ignatian directives. In relationship with the exercitant, the director must be involved but at the same time discreet; never seeking to do what the exercitant can do for him- or herself; never interposing between the Creator and his creature. In the image of an early *Directory*,[1] the 'exercises' are a 'supernatural birth', and the director's task is to provide the service of 'a skilled and conscientious midwife'.

---

[1] [The *Directories* are guidebooks intended to help the directors; they date from the time of Ignatius: see *On Giving the Spiritual Exercises; The Early Jesuit Manuscript Directories and the Official Directory of 1599*, translated and edited by Martin E. Palmer (St Louis: Institute of Jesuit Sources, 1996).]

Of the many who have written of the 'exercises' from a personal standpoint, few have described the experience as vividly as Ignatius's friend and commentator, Jerónimo Nadal. For years Nadal had vacillated over the question of joining Ignatius, and it was in order to reach a decision that he embarked on the 'exercises', which he made in 'a spacious room with a pleasant garden', procured for him by Ignatius, who feared his 'fits of melancholy'. Nadal recalls his experience as, with Fr Domenech[2] for director, he went into retreat on 5 November:

> I was in good heart though vexed with bad health and depression. In the first stages, I was all on fire for something out of the ordinary to happen to me, a vision, a revelation, a sign of some sort. I got fruit from the First Week and made a general confession to Fr Ignatius. In the Second Week I experienced even greater fruit ... but when I reached the election I became so perturbed and distracted that I could not keep either my mind or my body still. My mind was in darkness, my will sterile and obstinate, my body afflicted in head and stomach, and with a fever. I wrote down a great number of pros and cons, but I could reach no decision and remained so suspended that Fr Domenech was visibly depressed. On the seventeenth day he said that we must go ahead, as I had already wasted days on the election without result. I replied that I would like to devote one more night to it, and then I had a singular grace from God. I seized my pen and wrote as the Spirit of Christ moved me,

---

[2] [Jerónimo Domenech (1506–1593), from Valencia, joined the Society in 1540; later he was appointed Provincial of Sicily.]

with the utmost joy in my heart: 'In the name of the Most Holy Trinity, Father, Son and Hoy Ghost, I determine and propose to follow the evangelical counsels, with vows in the Society of Jesus'.[3]

Any student of the *Exercises* will recognise the main elements of this vivid little picture: an individual temperament with its own distinctive needs; the darkness and paralysis that so often precede the moment of breakthrough; the tension between the variables of individual progress and the constants of the charted Ignatian sequence; the role of the director, involved yet restrained, providing a living link between this particular retreatant and Ignatius's flexible methodology. Making the 'exercises', then, is a far cry from reading a text. The text in fact is a guidebook intended to help directors to place the lessons of Manresa at the service of people willing to learn the ways of God, as Ignatius did, in the school of experience.

The *Exercises* and the *Autobiography*

Plainly, Ignatius' story of his conversion has multiple implications for our understanding of the *Exercises*, which arose in their substance from this experience. Here two points in particular deserve to be highlighted.

First, while numerous and obvious parallels can be identified between the *Autobiography* and the *Exercises*, it becomes clear, on the most cursory inspection of the two

[3] [The original text of this account is available in the *Monumenta Historica Societatis Iesu, Epistolae et Monumenta Hieronymi Nadal*, volume 1, 17–18. For a recent account see William V. Bangert, *Jerome Nadal SJ, 1507–1580: Tracking the First Generation of Jesuits* (Chicago: Loyola, 1992), 22–26.]

documents, that the order and emphasis of the *Exercises* do not entirely correspond with those of Ignatius' story. The latter begins with a Second Time Election (Exx 176), made in the context of ideas to be worked out later in the Kingdom meditation (Exx 91–98), namely the following of Christ in the company of the heroic knights of Christ, dedicated to the Kingdom and to its 'more difficult tasks'. After that, the materials of the Second and Third Week contemplations appear inextricably interwoven with elements of the First Week. In the *Exercises*, these themes are reorganized into the step-by-step process of the 'Weeks', with the 'Election' finding its natural developmental place at the centre. In particular, the text of the First Week offers striking contrasts to Ignatius' own story. The point of closest similarity between the two is probably the vision of the Mother and Child, with its transformation of old sinful desires into 'disgust' (*asco*), clearly reminiscent of the First Week Triple Colloquy (Exx 62) and the petition for the grace of 'abhorrence' (*aborrecimiento*); but it is hard to say how far after this Ignatius remained in his own First Week. His spiritual 'crisis' does not fit naturally anywhere in the sequence of the *Exercises*, but in so far as 'scruples' are normally regarded as a typical First Week problem, Ignatius could be described as still in his First Week something like a year after his Election. Again, if that is so, the three-day General Confession was certainly not the sacramental rounding-off of the week commended in the *Exercises*.

In fact, one gets the impression from the *Autobiography* that the intensity of his prolonged initial fervour, coupled with his preoccupation with great penitential deeds, had the effect of retarding for

Ignatius the kind of First Week experience envisaged in the *Exercises*. At all events, the meditations of the First Week aim to introduce the retreatant into a far more ordered and focused journey along the 'purgative way' than Ignatius himself seems to have made. The retreatant must concentrate attention on the matter of the moment, without anticipation of later stages (Exx 11, the 11th Annotation). The fundamental grace—the shame and confusion which is something other than 'fear', and which has its basis in trust and gratitude—is proposed to the retreatant at the very outset. The Additions, while recommending penance, propose at the same time an attitude of moderation that Ignatius himself took so long to acquire.

Dissimilarities of this kind between the *Autobiography* and the *Exercises* bring out a feature of the latter often lost from view in facile statements about the 'experiential origin of the *Exercises*'. These are indeed based on Ignatius' experience at Manresa, but they do not attempt to reduplicate that experience. His experience is not so much the model for the *Exercises* as the raw material. The *Autobiography* casts light on the *Exercises* as a piece of creative spiritual pedagogy.

A second point is important, but delicate to handle. The *Autobiography* sheds light on Ignatian spirituality in general, and on the spirituality of the *Exercises* in particular, as *contemplative* in its tendency, and more specifically as characterised by a contemplative development of the Trinitarian and Christocentric dimensions similar in kind to that described by Ignatius. In speaking of a system or school of spirituality in this way one is not, of course, saying anything about what is necessarily going to happen to an individual who follows the school or system. The point at issue has to do with Ignatius' *expectations* of the way the Spirit might work in those who made the *Exercises*, and with the expectations built-in, as it were, to his system.

It is a commonplace of the history of Ignatian criticism that opinions have been divided on this matter. The character of the *Exercises* themselves is part of the problem. The *Exercises* are not a treatise on spiritual progress, but—precisely—a set of 'exercises'; and no 'exercise' could have, as its anticipated grace, a decisive mystical step of the kind associated with Ignatius' time of enlightenment. The material for prayer in the *Exercises* is always amenable to a restrictive interpretation: the Trinitarian exercises (the Incarnation contemplation and the Triple Colloquy) and the imaginative contemplations being seen as strictly limiting the retreatant to the kind of prayer Ignatius seem to have been making in the first stage of his own spiritual journey. If one remembers, too, the tendency in the past to distinguish sharply between 'mysticism' (an intrinsically extraordinary phenomenon mainly to be found in certain saints) and 'asceticism' (the way of the ordinary Christian), it is understandable that many authors should have concluded that the *Exercises* represent a purely 'ascetical' spirituality.[4]

On the other hand, there is much in the Annotations, Additions, Rules and other materials which suggests that, even on the basis of the text of the *Exercises*, this is an

---

[4] For example, Outram Evennett, *The Spirit of the Counter-Reformation* (Cambridge: Cambridge UP, 1968), sums up the *Exercises* as 'the systematised, *de-mysticised* quintessence of the process of Ignatius' own conversion and change of life', 45 (my italics).

over-simple reading. There is the 'direct communication between God and creature' (Exx 15, Annotation 15).[5] There is the 'consolation without preceding cause' (Exx 330, in the Rules for Discernment of the Second Week). There are the multiple allusions to 'taste', 'relish', etc. What is to be made of the Note which refers to the contemplation of the Second Week as 'an introduction and method to better and fuller contemplation later' (Exx 162)? In terms of spiritual evolution, what is the significance of the 'Contemplation to Attain Love', so strikingly different from imaginative contemplation in its presentation of God?

To interpret the spirituality of the *Exercises* they must be related to a wide and complex context. Their backdrop of the contemplative spirituality of the High Middle Ages is important. Heed must be taken of the Jesuit tradition expressed by Nadal, that Ignatius' Trinitarian contemplative gift is in some measure given to Jesuits in virtue of their vocation, and that the latter must therefore 'place the perfection of their prayer in contemplating the Trinity'. There is the 'mystical' interpretation of the *Exercises* represented, for example, by Cordeses at the end of the sixteenth century.[6] Among all this material, the *Autobiography* has its contribution to make, recounting as it does the development from which the *Exercises* spring—a development from Trinitarian

---

[5] This point was seen by an early critic of the *Exercises*, Pedroche, as proof of pure illuminism [compare John W. O'Malley, *The First Jesuits* (New Haven: Harvard UP, 1993), 43, 294; Joseph F. Conwell, *Walking in the Spirit: A Reflection on Jerónimo Nadal's Phrase 'Contemplative likewise in Action'* (St Louis: Institute of Jesuit Sources, 2003), 126–127].

[6] [Antonio Cordeses (1518–1601): his *Directory* is included in *On Giving the Spiritual Exercises*, document 32.]

devotional exercises and imaginative contemplation to the transitions that mark the period of enlightenment. This transition is presented in the *Autobiography* as integral to the spirituality of action and the world that gradually developed in the course of Ignatius' conversion. Certainly, Ignatius respected the gratuitousness of the action of God; he recognised that in his own experiences there was indeed something 'extraordinary'; he believed in the importance of solid foundations and proceeding step by step. It would be totally contrary to his mind to interpret the *Exercises* as a short cut to mysticism. On the other hand it is hard to see how an attentive reader of the *Autobiography*—unless affected by an *a priori* concept of mysticism as at any level rare and extraordinary—could be at ease with the view that it was Ignatius' intention to create a spiritual pedagogy based on the expectation that those making use of it would be led by the Spirit only half-way along the road he himself had travelled.

The Society of Jesus

A new form of religious life

The group of reformed priests and the fully fledged order that Ignatius left at his death are separated by long and involved administrative and legislative developments. Ignatius was no St Francis, idealistically remote from the crudities of legislation. For more than ten years he devoted himself with practical realism to the new and diversified needs that arose as his order grew. The result by the time of Ignatius' death was a rather more defined and regulated style of Jesuit life than that led by the first companions. *Constitutions* had been written (though they were not ratified till nearly two years later), and the hierarchical system of government, which he considered best suited both to the spirituality and the apostolate of the new order, had been established. The most ardent protagonist of Jesuit flexibility would have to admit that by 1556 no Jesuit residence would meet Pedro Ribadeneria's description of the companions' first Roman house as a place 'without constitutions or rules', and even without superior, 'since the few who were in the Society at that time all recognised Ignatius as their father'. Whether Ignatius always found the ideal legislative expression of the spirit of his youth is, as far as details are concerned, an endlessly debatable question; but the guiding principle of the whole legislative enterprise is clear. What Ignatius wanted was to enable the apostolic spirit and practical flexibility of the first companions to continue to flourish among men of more ordinary calibre than theirs, and in circumstances vastly more complex than they knew.

The Society was to be dedicated, then, to the same fundamental cause that had united the first companions: the service of Christ and of 'his Spouse, the Church'. In its expanding activities it would continue to work for 'the propagation of the faith and the teaching of Christian doctrine'. At the same time, following the precedent set by the first companions, commitment to the priestly ministry of the faith would carry its members beyond the limits of strictly priestly activity into a wider realm of Christian concern. Few religious founders can ever have entrusted their followers with so wide a mandate as the following description of what it is to be a member of the Society of Jesus:

He is a member of a society founded chiefly for this purpose: to strive especially for the defence and propagation of the faith and for the progress of souls in Christian life and doctrine, by means of public preaching, lectures and *any other ministration whatsoever of the word of God*, and further by means of the Spiritual Exercises, the education of children and unlettered persons in Christianity, and the spiritual consolation of Christ's faithful, through hearing confessions and administering the other sacraments. Moreover, this Society should show itself no less useful in reconciling the estranged, in holily assisting and serving those who are found in prisons and hospitals, and indeed in performing *any other work of charity*, according to what will seem expedient for the glory of God and the common good.[7]

A project of this scope and variety called for far-reaching changes in the style, and indeed the very concept, of religious life as it existed in the mid-sixteenth century. Mere modification of traditional details would not suffice. The very essentials of religious life—brotherhood, the observance of the counsels, the promotion and protection of the quality of personal life—all these would need to be reinterpreted in such a way that the communitarian and personal aspects of religious life would be neither accretions to, nor restraints upon, service, but constituents of it.

To see how this happens in practice, let us look at Ignatius' approach to two fundamental aspects of

[7] [A quotation from the *Formula of the Institute*, 6, available in *The Constitutions of the Society of Jesus*, translated by George E. Ganss (St Louis: Institute of Jesuit Sources, 1970), 66–67.]

religious life, namely formation and community—leaving till later his attitude[8] to the evangelical counsels, which belongs to the wider question of the order's underlying spirituality.

Formation

In legislating for the order's young members, Ignatius was guided by two needs, which were to some extent antithetical. First, each Jesuit must somehow personally appropriate the kind of experience from which the Society's ideals originally arose; and second, every Jesuit must become competent in the realm of theology. To meet the first of these needs, Ignatius devised the distinctive style of the Jesuit novitiate. In other religious orders at the time, the novitiate was a period of strict sequestration; its aim was to detach novices from the world and to provide an apprenticeship in monastic discipline and contemplation. The aim of Ignatius' novitiate is a little more complex:

> If someone enters a well-ordered monastery, he will be more separated from occasions of sin, because of the cloister, tranquillity and good order there than in our Society. We do not have that cloister, quiet and repose, but move about from place to place. Moreover, for someone with bad habits or some imperfection, a monastery so organized and ordered will suffice for him to perfect himself. But in our Society, it is necessary that one be extensively tested before being admitted. For as

---

[8] [This section is covered to some extent in the papers that were published in the collection, *Keeping in Touch*, edited by Joseph A. Munitiz (Leominster: Gracewing and Inigo, 2007).]

he travels about later on, he must associate with men and women, both good and bad. Such associations require greater strength and experience, as well as greater graces and gifts from God our Lord.[9]

The 'extensive testing' to which Ignatius refers takes place partly within the walls of the novitiate and partly in the outside world. When at home, the novice makes the Spiritual Exercises, and carries out the 'low and humble offices' well calculated to mortify an applicant of middle-class or aristocratic background. In the intervals he makes a month's pilgrimage, penniless and on foot; he teaches doctrine to children, he works in hospitals, and he gains experience in begging from door to door. More than an exercise in personal asceticism, this activity was a training for the ministry to come. Ignatius wanted the young members of his order to 'grow accustomed to discomfort in food and lodging', and to become 'disposed to do the same begging as they travel through the various regions of the world'. It was a system designed to develop and test the calling to be a contemplative in action.

Having thus been initiated into the first companions' experience of the apostolate, the young Jesuit must then embrace the quite different discipline of study, which had occupied so much of Ignatius' and the first companions' formative years. Esteem for learning, even a learning far beyond his own hard-won attainments, is so well-known a trait of Ignatius' personality that it is not always realised that he also regarded study as a rather

---

[9] [The idea, if not the exact words, to be found in Nadal, '6th Exhortation at Alcalá', 135, in *Monumenta Historica Societatis Iesu*, volume 90, Nadal volume 5, 368 (Rome, 1962).]

problematical element in Jesuit life, for in more ways than one it entailed departures from the norms of the apostolic calling. Houses of study needed, for instance, a financial regime permitting the security of fixed revenues. Moreover, the isolation of study, coupled with the rather desiccated character of the late scholasticism of the time, tended to produce a withering effect on the spirit. The direct ministry, as practised by the novice, could be relied upon to engender fervour; on the other hand, 'the occupation of the understanding with scholastic pursuits usually'—Ignatius believed—'brings on a certain interior dryness'. But for all that, so long as study was necessary —for the glory of God and the good of the neighbour— its claims were sacrosanct. Given that the student had experienced fervour in his novitiate experiments, and that after study he would have the opportunity to repeat those experiments in the 'Tertianship',[10] Ignatius was quite clear that during the student years a Jesuit gave glory to God through his books. In study he must find his mortification, his discipline, even a large part of his prayer; and Ignatius was adamant that he should be asked to carry only the minimum burden of devotional exercises.

Community life

What was Ignatius' approach to community life? As the history of the first companions might lead us to expect, it was an approach different in many respects from that of monasticism. As we might expect, too, Ignatius'

---

[10] [At the end of the main period of training, and thus after ordination, each Jesuit is expected to spend one year devoted mainly to spiritual training, in many ways a sort of second novitiate. As the first novitiate is itself divided into two periods, this final period is the 'third' (*tertius*), and hence called 'Tertianship'.]

concept is both distinctive and nuanced, bringing together a number of antithetical elements.

First of all, community for the Jesuit is not a place of insulation from the world, but a base from which he carries out an intensive activity within the world. As Nadal puts it with typical forthrightness:

> Whoever wants solitude and prayer by himself, whoever likes a hidden corner and getting away from men and dealing with them, is not for our vocation. For such a one there are the Carthusians and other institutes.[11]

It was not, then, the demands of community life that determined the scope of service, but the demands of service that determined the shape, style and spirit of community life. Ignatius lost no time in spelling out the practical implications of this. His first move towards establishing a new order had been to draw up a five-point statement of aims, in which an entire section was devoted to the suppression of choral office and statutory penances and to the need for Jesuits to cut back drastically on the elaborate liturgical ceremonies in vogue at the time. Choir, he argued, 'would take us away from the offices of charity to which we have entirely dedicated ourselves'. Celebrations must be simple and short, 'because we are frequently occupied a great part of the day, and even during the night, in caring for the sick in body and mind'. Obligatory penances—'fasts, disciplines, going about barefoot or with heads uncovered, distinct kinds of food, hair-shirts

---

[11] [Nadal, '3rd Exhortation at Alcalá', §83, in *Monumenta Historica Societatis Iesu*, volume 90, Nadal volume 5, 324 (Rome: Jesuit Historical Institute, 1962).]

or other corporal austerities'—might provide 'an excuse for withdrawing from the exercises we have proposed to ourselves'.

Similarly, Jesuit communities could not be tied down by highly detailed and standardised rules of the sort common in the traditional orders. To a large extent, Ignatius left it to local superiors to work out the rules for their own communities, in view of 'the times, persons and places of the different employments and houses'. The regulations actually drawn up, often under Ignatius' guidance and on the lines of the rules obtaining in the Roman houses, were admittedly highly numerous, and in many respects we would regard them today as needlessly fussy. Nevertheless, to the mind of Ignatius the distinction between *ad hoc* local rules and the *Constitutions* is clear; and the wide legislative framework of the latter was the only code binding on all Jesuits indiscriminately.

Yet for all this, Ignatius was far from depreciating the need for community life. While Jesuits might often work in isolation, he was insistent that they live in association. Ordinarily they belonged to established communities in colleges or residences; and even those picturesquely described as 'sent to produce fruit'—the frontier men who worked away from the base and lodged where opportunity offered—operated normally in pairs or threes.

How did Ignatius understand the nature and purpose of these groups? The community we glimpse in the provisions and admonitions of the *Constitutions* reflects, as any true community ideal must, the complexities of physical, psychological and religious need. It was a community, therefore, which must care for its sick, provide for material needs, and foster spiritual growth through encouragement and correction. On the other hand, even in its final and comparatively regulated form, Jesuit community life still embodies the unified apostolic vision of the first companions. The community has its specific internal commitments, but these are not something apart from, or additional to, service; they arise from the very nature of service 'in Christ', as Ignatius understood 'service'. The clue to this unity of service and community lies in Ignatius' concept of the overall objective of community, namely 'the union of minds and hearts'.

'Union', for Ignatius, was simultaneously a communitarian quality and an apostolic one. It was communitarian because, far from being a casually acquired by-product of work in the mission field, it could be forged only in the deliberate association of men open to the spirit and committed to one another. It was a quality of service because, as the *Deliberation of the First Fathers*[12] observed, 'spiritual power, like natural, is more effective when united than when fragmented into many parts'. In being dedicated to the ideal of union, Jesuit communities were directed simultaneously inwards and outwards: inwards, towards strengthening their own mutual ties; outwards, towards the service of their fellow men. Service, as Ignatius never let them forget, was the purpose for which they had been called into being; but service in Christ depended for its effectiveness on

---

[12] [This is the title of a document drawn up by the first companions, while they were discussing whether or not to adopt obedience as a vow: translated by Jules Toner, *Studies in the Spirituality of Jesuits*, 6/4 (1974).]

being done by men who genuinely loved one another and shared a common outlook.

But there is another consideration: while Jesuit community requires immediate association, it is not limited to the confines of a local group. One of the differences between Jesuit and monastic models of community is that the Jesuit model is two-dimensional: it encompasses both the local scene and the international body of the Society.

3 Ignatian Spirituality: Characteristic Features

IT IS IMPORTANT TO REALISE from the outset that the idea of 'characteristic features' in the spirituality of an individual or school easily incurs certain dangers. Christian spirituality is one before it is many, and if we become more preoccupied with what distinguishes than with what unites, we are liable to finish not so much with authentically distinctive spiritualities as with so many truncations of the gospel. A little reflection on what is sometimes said to distinguish lay, priestly and religious spiritualities, or the monastic and apostolic expressions of the latter, will show the dangers of pressing difference too far. Nevertheless, distinctiveness in spirituality is a fact. People and groups know, love and serve God in different ways. The differences are rooted ultimately in the varieties of vocation and gift. Their context consists in particular cultures, personalities, patterns of life experience. They express themselves externally in particular kinds of lifestyle, and inwardly in the esteem and search for different realms of spiritual experience. And these differences are in turn bound up with differences of language, imagery and theological emphasis. This variety contributes enormously to the richness of life, constituting a kind of prophetic network through which individuals and groups encourage, stimulate and challenge one another. So long, then, as we keep in mind that every authentic spirituality is in the end a way of living *one* faith in *one* God who reveals Himself in *one* Christ, and so long as we do not allow real differences to obscure what all authentic spiritualities hold in common, the study of an individual or school will necessarily focus on what is characteristic in that individual's contribution to the rich variety of Christian life.

God in all things

Perhaps the most fundamental characteristic of Ignatian spirituality consists in the indissoluble connection between our relationship to God in Himself and a profound involvement in what Nadal[1] calls 'all things, actions, and conversations', an involvement which is both a consequence of our relationship to God and a furtherance of it. But in order to understand this connection we must begin not with 'all things, actions and conversations', but with God. The spirituality of Ignatius is radically theocentric. He is a man of action, and in a very true sense a man of the world, because he is, first and foremost, a man of God.

Frequently recurring words in his vocabulary help us to specify what this means—to see who God is for Ignatius, and how he sees his relationship to God. He has a profound sense of divinity, of the 'goodness' of God. A dominant idea in his writing is that of 'glory'. God is the 'above', a term which is not so much spatial as hierarchical; God is above and beyond ourselves, our world, and anything we can do in his service. But God is also good, loving, the bestower of gifts—and the fundamental gift is to enable us to be God-centred.

[1] [See chapter 1, note 3 and chapter 2, note 3.]

To say that Ignatius is dominated by the divinity of God is to say that the God which is the centre of his life is *divine love*. If we were to falsify Ignatius' God by playing down His sheer divinity, we would falsify his sense of the divine; we would lose sight of the fact that divinity is 'love' and 'goodness' (kindness). And if a single word epitomizes Ignatius' response to God, it is the word 'love'. His love for God is ardent, affectionate, even familiar;[2] yet Ignatius is always conscious that what sounds like love can really be more superficial than it appears.

Two things in particular are necessary if our love for God is to be authentic. A true love for God is reverential: that is to say, God is to be loved precisely as transcendent. Tender love, even in a sense familiar love, never tries to possess God, to reduce Him to our human scale, to evacuate His mystery. However, even reverence is not enough, for reverence can degenerate to the level of the merely cultic, producing a love dominated too much by words, rather than deeds: a love characterizing a part of life, rather than the whole of it. Real *reverence* consists not just in the praise of God but in doing the will of God, which, Ignatius insists, is not just a matter of what one does, but of the orientation to God of the whole self, right down to the intimate core of intention.[3]

---

[2] [Clearly Michael intended to write more about the 'reciprocity' of the relationship of love: we make God 'happy' and 'grateful', and we 'contribute to His glory'.]

[3] [In a half-completed note Michael added that while 'reverence' is an attitude that would have been obviously culturally congenial to Ignatius, it is not in itself culturally adventitious; rather it is an integral element of all love.]

Love for God contains 'need-love'. We 'need' God for us to exist, to be happy, to be forgiven, and in the end to be saved. Indeed in the Principle and Foundation in the *Spiritual Exercises* (Exx 23), Ignatius speaks of the 'praise, reverence, and service of God' as 'means' to a personal end: to save my soul. But the Principle and Foundation is concerned to place the *Exercises* at the outset on the basis of a series of obvious and incontrovertible truths, and a sixteenth-century retreatant, even a self-centred and spiritually immature one, certainly felt the need to 'save his soul'.

But Ignatius goes beyond need-love. Though all is gift, the gifts of God include the gift to love God not for our own sakes alone, but for His. More audaciously than many, Ignatius uses the language of altruism when speaking of the love of God. A true love for God is generous and magnanimous: that God be praised, given pleasure, glorified, served, and that God receive me as a free gift—and God cannot have me as a gift unless I freely give myself. To describe Ignatius as radically 'theocentric' is to say that these are the concerns that dominate his life.

In action and in all things

It is this kind of radical relationship with God that Ignatius sees as being lived out *in action and in all things*. It must be noted at once that at one level finding God in action and in all things is a defining characteristic of Christian spirituality as such. Every tradition recognises that we find God as human beings, and in the activity and passivity of the human condition. Whether one is a hermit, an apostle, a layperson or whatever, one finds

God in the realms of mind, emotion, imagination and sense; in relationships with others; in interaction with the material world; and, of course, in the unsought sufferings of life. And if finding God will often be precisely in the asceticism of opposition, no authentic spirituality presses this point to the extent of writing off all created reality as impediment. In the dialectic between opposition and harmony, the thrust for those who seek God is towards harmony and reconciliation.

It will be clear from what has been said that whatever the special sense of 'action' for Ignatius, it does not mean that the sense of divine transcendence is lost; that God in a sense becomes absorbed into immediate realities; that our relationship with Him is implicit rather than explicit. And while it is true that Ignatius goes further than many in leading us to expect the experience of a positive, consoling harmony in activity, he does not give any grounds for the idea that this harmony can come about without asceticism in relation to the world. To find harmony, we need to encounter opposition. Growth in theocentricity requires the ordering to God of all that is not God, a continual *conversion* (a turning to), with its corollary of *aversion* (a turning from) in relation to everything in ourselves and the world which impedes us.

Conversion is radical. It is nothing less than turning the self inside out, coming to revolve around another centre of gravity. There is, therefore, in Christian growth a paradox: to find God in what is not God it is necessary to hold off what is not God. Since God is the Other-than-the-world, we only find Him as Other-than-the-world by being led into relations with the world, where we have to move beyond the claims of instinct and the immediately meaningful. All this is lived out in various ways, often in ways that, from a narrow religious standpoint, might not immediately suggest the idea of mortification or asceticism. But the human self, as spiritual and bodily, in its relations with others and the material world, is divided; and every Christian is involved in the deep asceticism through which alone we progress from dividedness to unity. It is impossible to read Ignatius even casually without becoming aware that the need for continual conversion, with its corollary of continual asceticism, is central to his spirituality.

The Jesuit way of life

To see why Ignatius (and the early Jesuits) saw their spirituality as particularly characterized by 'action' one has to look at the Jesuit way of life as the early Jesuits themselves looked at it. This means one must see it in the context of the prevailing idea among deeply religious people about what was the best way to lead a life completely committed to God. And in the sixteenth century, despite the degenerate state of the monastic ideal in practice, despite the existence for four centuries of the more open and exposed mendicant life, despite the strenuous opposition in certain critical circles to the very concept of monasticism, it remains true that the idea was still widespread that, if one wanted to live completely for God, the best way to do it was to live like a monk or a hermit. Essential to such a way of life is the systematic limitation of action and involvement in all things to strictly defined parameters, to ensure that, if possible, 'action' is only of a certain kind or intensity, and exposure to the world limited to physical separation. Jesuit life, too, has its limits, but they are understood in such a way that the place of 'action and all things' in Jesuit life is different from monasticism not only in fact, but in principle. The ideal of the monk is to shape life so that everything is ordered to his personal and communitarian commitment to prayer and penance. The Jesuit must find God in a life whose structure is ordered to the apostolate.

Ignatius lived out his life for God in circumstances in which activity, lack of space and seclusion, and exposure to the world were of a kind that others tended to see as an impediment to finding God. Indeed, it was in and through, not despite, the life he led, that he found God. That in this he differs from many of his time does not mean that he saw himself as somehow stronger than others. Nor, conversely, did he see others as graced to follow a purer and more perfect way to God. Rather he saw the matter in terms of 'gift', and of the importance of following one's own gift.

Theological infrastructure

Ignatius, as has been pointed out, was a 'theologian', not only in the sense that his studies had left him with a respectable academic competence, but in the sense that an important characteristic of his spirituality is the personal appropriation of truth, of faith-meaning. In order, therefore, to grasp a relationship with God which is so deeply involved in 'action and in all things' it is necessary to look at a number of theological emphases (one is not looking at more than emphases) that constitute his understanding of human activity and involvement in the world in relation to God.

To say that Ignatius loves God 'in Himself' is not to make God obscure His creation (so to speak), for God in Himself is creator and lord of all things. The phrase 'creator and lord' recurs again and again in his writings. It is no casual theological platitude, but a phrase charged with quite specific implications which dominate his outlook, and provide an essential key to understanding his spirituality. Creation is not for Ignatius located in the past; it is here-and-now reality.[4] The image it suggests is not static, but active ('God works and labours'). Ignatius emphasizes the purpose of God's work and labour, *viz.* human salvation and the fullness of the kingdom. The unfolding of this purpose is the 'glory of God'—'glory' for Ignatius being not the glory that belongs to God's being (which no action of ours can increase or diminish), but the coming about of God's purposes, and therefore a process. Hence to love God, to reverence Him, and to do His will, is to be involved in the unfolding of God's purposes, in His glory. In this one 'finds God' and experiences His enlightening, loving and strengthening presence. It would be too simple to say that 'finding God' in this sense is always chronologically the sequel to seeking or the reward for such seeking; what is true is that Ignatius never allows us to separate *finding* God from *seeking* him by involvement in his purposes.

---

[4] Ignatius has a strong sense of the world as coming *from* God, from God's initial act of creation, but to say that God is 'creator and lord' is to say that God is active here and now. [From incomplete notes.]

Service

This involvement in God's purposes is the key to Ignatius' central concept, 'service', by which he means all activity directly ordered to the transformation of the world into the kingdom of God: the winning back to God of everything under the thrall of the enemy of the human race. The work is God's, for only God can transform the *world* into the *kingdom*. But it is a work that God brings about through people, his 'servants', and to this service all men and women are in some way or other invited to participate. God entrusts the work of the kingdom, the 'glory' which consists in the realisation of that work, to people. If the work is all God's, it is also in a sense all theirs. To love and revere God, to do His will, to promote His glory, requires that we become involved in the wider reach of God's work. God commits us not only to our own salvation but to the salvation of others; and the world we must free from the enemy and bring under the domain of truth, love and justice is not only the world of our immediate circle but of human society. This approach to service, though wholly in line with the theology of apostolate in the Gospels and St Paul, places 'action' in a quite different frame of reference from that which was common among religious people in Ignatius's day.

Being in the world

There are three areas of our being in the world which everyone who seriously seeks God must recognise as both essential ways to God, and also possible obstacles.

The first is the *world*, whose immediacy so easily draws us away from ultimate reality. The second is *people*, for we have to recognise that instead of the love which is like the love of God we so easily love people in a way that competes with God.[5] The third is the *apostolate* itself, for we recognise that the work of God can so easily take precedence over our relationship with the God of the word.

If the first principle of Ignatius' theology of the *world* is the fact that it exists in order to help us to attain the end for which we are created, the second is that our relationship with the world is that of a 'user' of reality: 'It follows from this that the person has to use these things in so far as they help towards this end, and to be free of them in so far as they stand in the way of it' (Exx 23). In itself, the principle was not one which a person of Ignatius' time would wish to quarrel with; a statement remarkably like the one quoted is to be found in the *Enchiridion* of Erasmus.[6] So, again, it is not the idea that is characteristic of Ignatius, but the way he assimilates it and lives out its implications. Though the world exists to 'help' us achieve our salvation, there is no momentum in things that automatically carries one to God. Everything depends on the way one 'uses' things—the patterns of use and avoidance one freely chooses to adopt in relation to things.[7] The criterion of choice is God's will and what makes for His glory; and

---

[5] [Unfortunately pages are missing here, and it is likely that they contained reflections on the importance and dangers of personal relationships.]

[6] [Desiderius Erasmus (1466/9–1536), the outstanding humanist of his day; Ignatius' attitude to his works is greatly disputed as there are striking similarities and differences between them: compare O'Malley, *The First Jesuits*, 260–264.]

[7] A 'means-and-ends' language can suggest a kind of spiritual pragmatism, as opposed to the fusion of the experience of God in immediate meanings. [Another incomplete note, which would probably have been expanded.]

the will of God is sometimes found within what is immediately meaningful and sometimes in defiance of this. This subordination of the uses of reality to the will of God imposes a stringent asceticism, but the asceticism of use is a slightly different asceticism from the asceticism of subjection to established patterns, which leave little room for choice. It is also different from the asceticism which looks at the world mainly as an obstacle, and sees involvement with it as something as far as possible to be avoided. Certainly for Ignatius, choices are made within the established and permanent patterns of a way of life. But for him God-directed choice has a larger role in spirituality than it has in classic monasticism. And while Ignatius insists on a positive preference for the paradoxical ways of God, in the end the fundamental question that he asks of any reality is not, 'Can I avoid this?' but, 'Does God want me to use this, and if so, how?'

The apostolate and the mystical

Ignatius' spirituality consists in a personal relationship with God, which is at the same time a relationship of service in the world. The service does not override the personal element, yet the personal is totally permeated by the implications of service. Given the scale of action and its implications, this must be so: action invades the inner world.

All the themes of traditional spirituality are transposed into an apostolic key, even those which are most personal and, in a sense, 'interior': prayer, mortification, poverty, obedience, etc. In view of a particular difficulty posed by Ignatius, when compared with other spiritual masters, one implication in particular of the apostolic character of Ignatian spirituality merits special attention: in what sense can the term 'mysticism' be applied to his apostolic attitude?

Though Ignatius reveals little of his own spiritual journey, it is quite clear from the surviving sheets of his *Spiritual Journal*[8] that Ignatius himself was a highly endowed Trinitarian mystic. Yet to read these pages with the doctrine of, say, John of the Cross or *The Cloud of Unknowing* in mind, is to find oneself in a realm which in many respects fails to fit the classic picture of the higher levels of mystical union. Even in his mature mysticism, Ignatius is imaginative, emotional, and uses 'methods'; sense responses, especially tears, loom large.

When one turns from the evidence of his own experience to the way he talks about mysticism—or, more accurately, does not talk about it—the impression is given that Ignatius was not only a rather untypical mystic, but that, whatever is to be said about his own mysticism, he seems to play down the mystical in his doctrine to others. He warns against the hazards of long prayer and of the quest for withdrawal. His stress is laid rather on the importance of giving priority to the claims of *action* over those of experiences only available in withdrawn prayer. He takes no interest in the scale of progress. The *Exercises* make the impression, even on careful and informed readers, of being totally bereft of properly mystical teaching.

The impression of Ignatius as an anti-mystic in his teaching comes partly from his language. While,

---

[8] [Easily available in St Ignatius of Loyola, *Personal Writings*.]

obviously, he does not use the word 'mysticism', the significance of phrases like 'finding God', 'consolation without preceding cause', 'direct communication between Creator and creature', have tended not to receive from commentators the attention they deserve. Yet it remains true that there is much in what he does say to suggest that he discouraged interest in the mystical, and that perhaps explains why he has no very significant place in the literature of mysticism.

In fact, all these things are part of Ignatius' contribution to the study of mysticism. He stands against those who see genuine mysticism only in the radically negative or apophatic tradition, that is, those who think that because mystical love and knowledge are beyond imagination, emotion, the senses, one should recognise the mystical only when they are all completely (or nearly) absent. He stands with all genuine mystical writers—but more explicitly than many of them—against the cult of the mystical for itself or as a kind of status, or an unhealthy interest in plotting the 'stages' of one's progress. More strongly than many, he stresses the dangers of 'illuminism'. He discourages a preoccupation with mystical 'states' that overlooks the importance of 'moments'. But such warnings will inevitably suggest an overall negative attitude towards the mystical, if they are seen as coming from a teacher who is not interested in mysticism or who positively discourages it. And it is in this presupposition that they are frequently interpreted.

As well as Ignatius' language—and his silences— there is another reason for this: the assumption that real mysticism essentially belongs to the 'desert', and that it is essentially incompatible with the involvement in ministry and the world that characterizes the Ignatian apostolic life. Yet it is precisely this *a priori* assumption, already challenged by the Dominicans in the twelfth century, that Ignatius challenges afresh.

Undoubtedly there is a kind of mystical encounter that does require the conditions of the desert. This position, borne out by centuries of experience, is a large part of the basis of the enclosed or withdrawn life, and Ignatius certainly does not quarrel with it. Indeed, he insists that some people are given graces for the desert, and others graces for helping their neighbour. It is as a grace of the latter kind that Nadal sees the grace so characteristic of Ignatius, and given in some measure to all Jesuits 'in virtue of our vocation', to be 'contemplative in action'.[9] One can recognise in Ignatius' own experience, and in his teaching and the teaching of his companions, an 'apostolic mysticism', a mysticism of involvement in the work of the Trinity in the world.

Service of God in the world

The key to understanding Ignatian mysticism consists in seeing the mystical not simply as a quality of Ignatius' personal relationship to God, abstracting from his vocation to service, but as the quality of a relationship to God which is one of involvement in the service of God in the world. Because Ignatius is called to service in a particular and strong sense, the more his relationship

---

[9] [In notes commenting on the *Examen*, a sort of 'preface' to the *Constitutions*, Nadal describes Ignatius as *contemplativus simul in actione* ('contemplative also in action'): compare Bangert, *Jerome Nadal*, 214–215.]

to God enters the realm of the mystical, the more completely and effectively he is a servant. Thus his mysticism can be characterized as a mysticism of service[10] not just in the sense that authentic mysticism will always have service of some kind as its consequence, but in the sense that Ignatius represents a mysticism that has service as its object. This does not mean that Ignatius confuses prayer and action; he recognises, as every contemplative recognises, that in passing from prayer to action there is a sacrifice to be made. But it is the mystical itself that compels him to make the sacrifice and renders him incapable of resting content with the union of prayer; for the God who gives Himself to the apostle in contemplation is the 'working God', who involves the apostle in His own action in the world.

Ignatius recognises the quite specific quality of the encounter with God that comes about in the prayer of withdrawal, and in his prayer the apostolic mystic is not always consciously concerned with action. Yet more than others, Ignatius recognises that life and its concerns will enter into prayer, as the apostle seeks to 'discern' the will of God in a concrete decision. But though he insists that the mystical comes into focus only in moments of withdrawn prayer, he also insists that of its nature it extends into action and becomes a quality of life. Mysticism energizes action with the power of the Spirit. It illuminates action, enabling the apostle in his action to see, judge and act with the mind of Christ. It enables him or her to find God in all things,

---

[10] [As pointed out by Joseph de Guibert (who is mentioned in Michael's notes at this point): compare *The Jesuits*, 178–181.]

giving the wisdom that consists in 'seeing all things in their natural relationship with God'.[11] Because the mystical gifts of the apostle are in themselves 'apostolic', their effects on the person are in a a sense apostolically appropriate. It is a characteristic of Ignatian mysticism that it unites to God not only the 'spiritual faculties' of mind and will, but 'bodily faculties, such as memory and imagination', which refer to action.[12]

[11] [A phrase attributed to St Thomas Aquinas.]
[12] [de Guibert, *The Jesuits*, 55.]